ST. JOHN OF GOD DEVOTIONAL NOVENA PRAYER

NEW EDITION 2024

BY

MAXWELL L. JOHN

COPYRIGHT @ 2024

Table of Contents

INTRODUCTION TO NOVENA 5
PURPOSE AND IMPORTANCE OF THE NOVENA 11
DAY 1: SEEKING ST. JOHN OF GOD'S INTERCESSION 17
DAY 2: EMBRACING COMPASSION AND CHARITY 23
DAY 3: SURRENDERING TO GOD'S WILL 28
DAY 4: SERVING THOSE IN NEED '................... 33
DAY 5: STRENGTHENING FAITH AND HOPE 38
DAY 6: HEALING AND COMFORT - OPENING PRAYER 43
DAY 7: UNITING IN PRAYER 48
Day 8: Gratitude And Thanksgiving 53
DAY 9: TRUSTING IN DIVINE PROVIDENCE 57
CONCLUSION AND CLOSING PRAYER 62

INTRODUCTION TO NOVENA

BACKGROUND OF ST. JOHN OF GOD

EARLY LIFE:

St. John of God, also known as João Cidade (Juan Ciudad in Spanish), was born on March 8, 1495, in Montemor-o-Novo, Portugal, at a period of significant political and social upheaval in Europe. He was born into a devoted Catholic household, yet his upbringing was filled with hardships. At the age of eight, he lost his father, and his mother battled to support him and his siblings.

Youth and Military Service:

In his youth, John was restless and eager for adventure. He left home at the age of eight to work as a shepherd, and eventually became a young soldier, participating in Charles V's military exploits as Holy Roman Emperor. His military duty exposed him to the ugliness of battle and the hardships that troops suffer, informing his subsequent devotion to compassion and service.

Religious conversion:

At the age of 40, after years of traveling and soul-searching, John had a deep religious conversion. The famed Spanish priest and mystic, John of Avila, delivered a sermon that sparked this transition. John of God, filled with guilt for his previous crimes and inspired by the message of repentance and divine mercy, chose to devote his life to serving God and his fellow humans.

Service in Granada:
Following his conversion, John of God relocated to Granada, Spain, where he began his extraordinary path of service to the ill and poor. He first worked as a shepherd and then as a bookshop, spending his money to help the impoverished. Deeply touched by the suffering he observed among the sick and destitute, John of God felt

compelled to act.

Establishment of Hospital and Religious Order:

In 1539, inspired by a sermon on the Feast of St. Sebastian, John of God established a tiny hospital in Granada to care for the ill and needy. Despite several hurdles, including hostility from authorities and criticism from people who questioned his motivations, John of God remained committed to his goal. He gathered disciples who shared his vision of compassionate care, and together they founded the Order of the Brothers Hospitallers of St. John of God, generally known as the Hospitaller

Order of St. John of God.

Charism and legacy:
St. John of God's charism revolved around hospitality, compassion, and unselfish care to the ill and underprivileged. He welcomed individuals from all walks of life, regardless of social class or background, and treated them with compassion and decency. His commitment to the ill was marked by personal humility, hard effort, and a firm belief in divine providence.

Death and canonization:
St. John of God died on March 8, 1550, at the age of 55, after falling

while assisting in the transportation of a sick man. He was made a saint by Pope Alexander VIII on October 16, 1690, and his feast day is March 8th. St. John of God is honored as the patron saint of hospitals, the sick, nurses, firemen, and alcoholics.

Legacy and Influence:
St. John of God's legacy lives on via the Hospitaller Order, which he founded and now maintains hospitals, nursing homes, and other healthcare institutions all over the world. His example of love, compassion, and service continues to inspire many people and organizations who care for the ill and downtrodden, symbolizing

the eternal message of Christian charity and unity.

PURPOSE AND IMPORTANCE OF THE NOVENA

A novena to St. John of God serves several reasons, all of which revolve around asking his intercession, improving one's spirituality, and emulating his virtues. The significance of this novena stems from its capacity to build a closer relationship with St. John of God and gain inspiration from his life and actions.

1. Seeking Intercession: The major goal of the novena is to invoke the intercession of St. John of God. Believers look to him as a strong

advocate before God, asking for assistance in times of need, particularly in concerns of disease, healthcare, charity, and compassion. St. John of God's excellent life of service and reputation for delivering miracles make him an appealing figure for intercession.

2. Spiritual Growth: A novena is a spiritual discipline in which members set aside time each day for prayer, thought, and contemplation. The novena's planned prayers and thoughts can help people improve their relationship with God, grow in faith, and strengthen their spiritual determination.

3. Virtues that St. John of God exemplified were compassion, selflessness, humility, and faith in divine providence. The novena allows members to ponder on these qualities and attempt to embody them in their own lives. Individuals are encouraged to conduct more charitable and service-oriented lives after reflecting on St. John of God's example.

4. Communal Prayer: Novenas are frequently prayed together, either in a church or among a community of believers. Coming together in prayer promotes a sense of togetherness and solidarity among participants. The shared experience of prayer for a

common purpose, such as asking the intercession of St. John of God, deepens Christians' relationships of solidarity and mutual support.

5. Novenas have a long history in Catholic spirituality and devotional practice. They are a beloved method of prayer that has been passed down through generations of believers. Participating in a novena for St. John of God lets people to engage with this rich tradition while also expressing their devotion to this great saint.

In summary, the novena to St. John of God seeks intercession, promotes spiritual growth, exemplifies virtues, fosters community via communal prayer, and honors a beloved devotional tradition. Its significance stems from its potential to develop one's faith, take inspiration from the life of St. John of God, and foster a stronger dedication to serve others in the spirit of love and compassion.

DAY 1: SEEKING ST. JOHN OF GOD'S INTERCESSION

Opening Prayer:

Begin the first day of the novena by assembling in prayer. Find a peaceful, comfortable place where you may concentrate your thoughts and objectives.

Begin with the Sign of the Cross, a solemn gesture representing the oneness of the Father, Son, and Holy Spirit.

As you begin this novena devoted to St. John of God, pray to the Holy Spirit for direction, discernment, and an open heart.

2. Reflections on St. John of God's Life:

Spend some time reflecting on the life and legacy of St. John of God. Consider his astonishing transformation from a life of worldly interests to one solely committed to aiding the ill and underprivileged. Reflect on his tremendous compassion, humility, and unshakeable faith in God's providence, which guided him through his charitable mission.

3. Novena Prayer for Day One:

On this first day of the novena, pray specifically to St. John of God for his intercession for your objectives. Address St. John of God directly, expressing your faith in his divine help and requesting his assistance in your time of need.

You might utilize a traditional prayer dedicated to St. John of God or write your own personal plea, expressing your goals with honesty and trust.

4. Personal Reflection:

After the official prayer, spend some

time for personal thought.
Consider any specific intentions or prayers you want to convey to St. John of God during this novena.
Consider how St. John of God's example of unselfish devotion and strong faith might inspire and lead you through your own life and challenges.

5. Closing prayer:

Finish the first day of the novena with a closing prayer, thanking St. John of God for his intercession and recognizing his presence in your prayers.

Express thankfulness for the chance to seek his divine aid, and request ongoing direction and support throughout the novena's remaining days.

End with a final invocation of the Sign of the Cross, which represents your confidence in the Triune God and your reliance on St. John of God's intercession.

6. Optional devotional practice:

Consider burning a candle or putting an icon of St. John of God prominently to serve as a visual reminder of your prayers and intentions throughout the novena. This practice can serve as concrete evidence of your commitment to seeking the intercession of St. John of God and a focal point for your daily prayers.

DAY 2: EMBRACING COMPASSION AND CHARITY

Opening Prayer:

Begin the second day of the novena with a devout spirit. Invoke the Holy Spirit to direct your thoughts and open your heart to the virtues of compassion and charity.
Sign yourself with the Cross, which represents your trust in the Triune God and your willingness to accept divine favor.

2. Reflections on St. John of God's Acts of Charity:

Take some time to ponder on the life of St. John of God, particularly his deeds of compassion and generosity. Consider how selflessly St. John of God cared for the ill, the impoverished, and the disenfranchised, reflecting Christ's compassion through his devotion to others.

Consider how his example motivates you to practice greater compassion and generosity in your own life.

3. Novena Prayer for Day Two:

Offer a special prayer to St. John of God, expressing your wish to emulate his qualities of compassion and generosity.

Ask for his intercession to help you develop a compassionate heart and a charitable attitude toward people in need.

You can perform a conventional prayer to St. John of God or write your own personal petition centered on the themes of compassion and charity.

4. Personal Reflection:

Following the formal prayer, take a few moments for personal meditation. Consider your own potential for compassion and kindness. Consider how you might emulate St. John of God by reaching out to individuals who are suffering or in need. Determine what particular activities you may take to express compassion and charity in your everyday life.

5. Closing prayer:

End the second day of the novena with a concluding prayer, praising St. John of God for his example and intercession.

Ask for his continuing direction and aid as you work to embody compassion and charity in your thoughts, words, and actions.

Finish with a final invocation of the

Sign of the Cross, reinforcing your faith and confidence in God's mercy to help you develop these virtues.

DAY 3: SURRENDERING TO GOD'S WILL

Opening Prayer:

As I/We begin the third day of the novena with a prayerful attitude, asking the Holy Spirit to guide your thoughts and help you yield to God's desire.
Make the Sign of the Cross to express your receptivity to divine favor and faith in God's providence.

A reflection on St. John of God's faith in God:

Consider St. John of God's life, concentrating on his unshakable faith in God's plan.

Consider the problems and obstacles St. John of God encountered when assisting the ill and destitute, as well as how he entirely yielded to God's direction and providence.

Consider how St. John of God's example of submission might encourage you to trust God's plan for your life.

Novena Prayer for Day Three:

Offer a specific prayer to St. John of God, expressing your willingness to submit to God's will.

Request St. John of God's intercession to help you abandon control and believe in God's perfect plan for your life.

You might utilize a conventional prayer dedicated to St. John of God or write your own personal petition centered on the topic of surrender.

Personal Reflection:

Following the formal prayer, allow time for personal meditation. Consider the areas of your life in which you struggle to yield to God's will. Consider any worries, doubts, or wants that are preventing you from fully trusting God.

Determine what measures you may take to develop a stronger feeling of surrender and faith in God's plan.

Closing prayer:

End the third day of the novena with a concluding prayer, praising St. John of God for his example of surrender and intercession on your behalf. Ask for his continual advice and aid as you work to fully surrender to God's will in your life.

Finish with a final invocation of the Sign of the Cross to reaffirm your faith and confidence in God's providence.

DAY 4: SERVING THOSE IN NEED '

Opening Prayer:

Begin the fourth day of the novena with a prayerful attitude, requesting the Holy Spirit to direct your thoughts and inspire your heart to help those in need.
Sign yourself with the Cross to demonstrate your commitment to following in the footsteps of St. John of God and serving others with compassion and love.

Reflection on St. John of God's Care for the Sick:

Consider the life of St. John of God, particularly his dedication to the ill, destitute, and oppressed.

Consider St. John of God's compassionate caring for people in need, which frequently required significant personal sacrifice.

Consider how St. John of God's example of service might motivate you to help others who are suffering and in need.

Novena Prayer for Day Four:

Offer a special prayer to St. John of God, expressing your wish to emulate his example and help people in need with compassion and charity.

Seek St. John of God's intercession to help you notice and react to the needs of others with compassion and empathy.

You might utilize a conventional prayer dedicated to St. John of God or write your own personal petition centered on the topic of helping people in need.

Personal Reflection:

Following the formal prayer, allow time for personal meditation. Consider how you may include acts of

service into your regular routine.
Consider your particular abilities and resources, and how you may utilize them to help others.
Identify chances in your neighborhood or surrounds to make a good difference by helping people in need.
Closing prayer:

Finish the fourth day of the novena with a concluding prayer, thanking St. John of God for his example of unselfish devotion and intercession on your behalf.
Ask for his continuing direction and aid as you endeavor to embody his values and serve those in need with

compassion and love.

Finally, invoke the Sign of the Cross to reaffirm your resolve to following in St. John of God's footsteps.

DAY 5: STRENGTHENING FAITH AND HOPE

Opening Prayer:

Begin the fifth day of the novena with a prayerful attitude, asking the Holy Spirit to direct your thoughts and increase your trust and hope. Sign yourself with the Cross, indicating your reliance on God's grace and faith in St. John of God's intercession.

Reflections on St. John of God's Faith and Hope

Consider the life of St. John of God, particularly his unshakable confidence and optimism in God's providence. Consider the problems and obstacles St. John of God had throughout his journey to serve the ill and destitute, as well as how his faith helped him through tough times.

Consider how St. John of God's example of faith and hope might encourage you to believe in God's plan and be hopeful in the face of hardship.

Novena Prayer for Day Five:

Offer a specific prayer to St. John of

God, expressing your wish to deepen your trust and hope in God.

Request St. John of God's intercession to help you believe in God's providence and remain optimistic, especially in tough times.

You might utilize a conventional prayer dedicated to St. John of God or write your own passionate petition centered on the themes of faith and hope.

Personal Reflection:

Following the formal prayer, allow time for personal meditation. Consider the areas of your life in

which you struggle to preserve trust and hope. Consider any concerns, anxieties, or uncertainties that you may be experiencing on your spiritual path.
Identify ways to deepen your faith and hope, such as via prayer, scripture reading, and devotion.

Closing prayer:

Close the fifth day of the novena with a prayer of thanksgiving to St. John of God for his example of trust and hope, as well as his intercession on your behalf.
Ask for his continuing direction and

aid as you work to grow your faith and remain optimistic in God's promises.

Finish with a final invocation of the Sign of the Cross, confirming your faith in God's providence and resolve to following in the footsteps of St. John of God.

DAY 6: HEALING AND COMFORT - OPENING PRAYER

Begin the sixth day of the novena with a prayerful attitude, asking the Holy Spirit to direct your thoughts and offer healing and consolation to those in need.
Sign yourself with the Cross to express your faith in God's healing power and dependence on St. John of God's intercession.

Thoughts on St. John of God's Miracles:

Consider the miracles credited to St.

John of God during his lifetime and afterward.

Consider the healing and comforting stories related with St. John of God's intercession, as well as how his compassion and dedication alleviated suffering.

Consider how St. John of God's example of healing and consolation might motivate you to pray for individuals who are in need of physical, emotional, or spiritual healing.

Novena Prayer for Day Six:

Make a particular prayer to St. John

of God, requesting his intercession for healing and consolation for yourself and others.

Seek St. John of God's assistance in bringing relief to people who are sick, suffering, or in distress, and pray for their bodily, emotional, and spiritual well-being.

You might utilize a conventional prayer dedicated to St. John of God or write your own personal petition centered on the themes of healing and consolation.

Personal Reflections:

Following the formal prayer, allow

time for personal meditation.

Consider those in your life who are in need of healing and consolation.

Consider their individual needs and concerns, and lift them in prayer to St. John of God.

Consider how you might be a source of healing and consolation in the lives of others by demonstrating compassion, understanding, and spiritual support.

Closing Prayer:

Close the sixth day of the novena with a prayer of thanksgiving to St. John of God for his example of healing and consolation, as well as his intercession on behalf of people in need.

Ask for his continuing wisdom and aid as you work to offer healing and comfort to others in your life and community.

Finally, invoke the Sign of the Cross to reaffirm your faith in God's healing power and resolve to following in St. John of God's footsteps.

DAY 7: UNITING IN PRAYER

Opening Prayer:

Begin the seventh day of the novena with a prayerful spirit, understanding the power and significance of unified prayer.
Sign yourself with the Cross, indicating your oneness with other Christians and your faith in St. John of God's Intercession.

Reflections on the Power of Prayer:

Consider the value of prayer as a tool for uniting believers and seeking

God's love and direction.
Consider the biblical instances of community prayer, as well as the Catholic faith's rich prayer heritage. Consider how combined prayer develops links of solidarity and increases the power of intercession.

Novena Prayer for Day Seven:

Offer a special prayer to St. John of God, asking for his intercession on behalf of all novena participants' intentions.
Pray for unity among Christians, asking St. John of God to assist in uniting hearts in prayer and bringing

up the concerns of the community. You might utilize a conventional prayer dedicated to St. John of God or write your own personal petition centered on the idea of unity in prayer.

Personal Reflections:

Following the formal prayer, allow time for personal meditation. Consider the value of praying for others and working together in intercession for common objectives and intents.

Consider how you might actively join in coordinated prayer activities in your town and beyond.

Closing Prayer:

End the seventh day of the novena with a closing prayer, thanking St. John of God for his intercession and the chance to pray alongside other Christians.
Ask for his continuing guidance and aid in improving your prayer life and sense of community with others. Finish with a final invocation of the Sign of the Cross, reinforcing your confidence in God's presence and your will to continue praying with

others.

Day 8: Gratitude And Thanksgiving

Opening Prayer

Begin the eighth day of the novena with a prayer of thankfulness, thanking God's benefits and requesting St. John of God's intercession.
Sign yourself with the Cross, expressing thankfulness for the gift of faith and the ability to give thanks.

Reflections on Gratitude:

Consider the significance of creating a spirit of thankfulness in your life.

Consider the large and little benefits you have received from God and others.
Consider how thankfulness may change your view and attitude, promoting joy and fulfillment.

Novena Prayer for Day Eight:

Offer a special prayer of gratitude to St. John of God for his intercession throughout the novena.
Express thanks for St. John of God's inspiration and guidance on your spiritual path.
Thank you to St. John of God for setting an example of selflessness and

compassion, as well as for his ongoing intercession on behalf of people in need.

Personal Reflections:

Following the formal prayer, allow time for personal meditation.
Reflect on the specific benefits and graces you experienced throughout the novena.
Consider how thankfulness has strengthened your connection with God and others, and how you might maintain an attitude of thanksgiving in your everyday life.

Closing Prayer:

Finish the eighth day of the novena with a prayer of appreciation to God and St. John of God for their love and kindness.

Ask for the grace to be grateful in all situations, acknowledging God's providence and benefits in every part of your life.

Finally, make the Sign of the Cross to demonstrate your confidence and trust in God's ongoing benevolence.

Day

DAY 9: TRUSTING IN DIVINE PROVIDENCE

Opening Prayer:

Begin the ninth day of the novena in prayer, submitting to God's providence and seeking the direction of the Holy Spirit.
Sign yourself with the Cross to express your faith in God's loving care and dependence on St. John of God's intercession.

Thoughts on Trusting in Divine Providence:

Consider the notion of divine providence, and acknowledge God's caring and guiding presence in your life.

Consider how God has supplied for you in the past, even in tough situations, and how He continues to guide you on your spiritual journey. Consider how St. John of God's unshakable faith in divine providence helped him through times of struggle and uncertainty.

Novena Prayer for Day Nine:

Offer a specific prayer to St. John of God, expressing your wish to place your whole confidence in God's providence.

Ask for St. John of God's intercession to help you relinquish your anxieties and fears to God, believing in His perfect plan for your life.

You might utilize a conventional prayer dedicated to St. John of God or write your own personal plea centered on the topic of faith in divine providence.

Personal Reflections:

Following the formal prayer, allow time for personal meditation. Consider the areas of your life in which you struggle to believe in God's providence. Consider any worries, doubts, or uncertainties that may be impeding your capacity to submit to God's will.

Determine what measures you may take to develop a stronger sense of trust and surrender in your relationship with God.

Closing Prayer:

Finish the ninth day of the novena with a concluding prayer, praising St. John of God for his example of faith in divine providence and intercession on your behalf.

Ask for his continuing direction and aid as you work to strengthen your faith in God's loving care and providential leadership.

Finish with a final invocation of the Sign of the Cross to reaffirm your faith and confidence in God's providence.

CONCLUSION AND CLOSING PRAYER

As we complete our novena to St. John of God, let us reflect on the inspiration we have gained from his life and example. Throughout these nine days of prayer, we have sought St. John of God's intercession, reflecting on his qualities of compassion, humility, and faith in divine Providence. We've surrendered our intentions to him, asking for his assistance in times of need and aspiring to mirror his unselfish compassion for others.

May St. John of God's example

continue to encourage us on our own religious journeys. May his unrelenting commitment to helping those in need motivate us to provide love and compassion to everyone who crosses our way. And may his faith in divine providence inspire us to give our anxieties and fears to God, believing in His perfect plan for our life.

As we end this novena, let us remain committed to the teachings we have learned and the prayers we have given. May God's mercy, through the intercession of St. John of God, continue to lead and sustain us in all our activities.

Closing prayer:

Dear Heavenly Father,

We appreciate the donation of this novena dedicated to St. John of God. We have sought your grace and direction via his intercession, placing our wishes in your loving care. As we complete these nine days of prayer, we beg for the strength to walk in St. John of God's footsteps, living lives of compassion, humility, and faith in your divine providence.

St. John of God, who spent his life to aiding the ill and destitute, we come to you in our hour of need. Pray for us, so that we might be motivated by your example to reach out with love and compassion to everyone who is suffering. Help us to put our confidence in God's plan for our lives, releasing our anxieties and fears into His loving care.

Lord, we offer you our prayers and intentions, confident that you will hear and respond according to your will. May the grace of this novena continue to bless our lives, increasing our faith and growing our love for you and one another.

We beg this through Christ, our Lord. Amen.

Made in United States
North Haven, CT
27 July 2025